OMNIBUS PRESS
PRESENTS

THE STORY OF
PEARL JAM

D0746733

Copyright © 1993, 1996 Omnibus Press
(A Division of Book Sales Limited)

Edited by Chris Charlesworth
Book designed by Studio Twenty
Picture research by David Brolan
Updated by Kalen Rogers
Cover designed by Amy MacIntyre

ISBN 0.8256.1572.0
Order No. OP 47858

Exclusive Distributors:
Book Sales Limited
8/9 Frith Street, London W1V 5TZ England

Music Sales Corporation
257 Park Avenue South, New York, NY 10010 USA

Music Sales Pty. Limited
120 Rothschild Street, Rosebery, Sydney,
NSW 2018, Australia

Photo Credits
Text pages: All Action, Edie Baskin/Retna,
Anita Bugge/SIN, Greg Freeman/SIN,
Steve Gillett/Redferns, London Features International,
Steve Pumphrey/Retna,
Relay Photos, RIP/Retna,
Chris Taylor/Retna,
Neils van Iperon/Retna
Update photo credits:
Front cover: Kelly A. Swift/Retna
Back cover: Steve Gullick/Retna
pgs 48 & 49: Kristin Callahan/Retna
p.50: A.J. Barratt/Retna
p.51: Armando Gallo/Retna
pgs 52 & 56: Kevin Mazur/LFI
p.53 T. Stone/Retna
p.54: Steve Granitz/Retna
p.55: Joe Hughes/LFI
p.57: Kevin Cummins/LFI
pgs 58 & 59: Jake Blakesberg/Retna
pgs 60 & 61: Jake Blakesberg/Retna
pgs 62 & 63: Kevin Mazur/LFI
pg 64: Amy Rachlin/Retna

OMNIBUS PRESS
London • New York • Paris • Sydney

Pearl Jam

To think all this started 7 years ago…

The Stone Faction

(Funny City Rock Guy with a Marshall)

Meets the Jeff faction

(serious Montana skate punk with a basketball)

Green River

3 records. 3 tours. The Seattle Sound sub pop loud. Long hair. Etc…
…mainly Etc.

One thing didn't lead to another and they left.

Mother Love Bone.

2 records. 1 tour… Love Rock. Lots of promise. Talk. Hype.

Then, Andy left to go do his solo record.

Once again, the Stone & Jeff Faction opt out 2 do a new thang.

Mookie Blaylock… Reeenk Roink…

Pearl Jam…

3 new guys. The Kiss ass function.

EDDIE…
(Master of words. Earth Guru).

DAVE…
(Percussive God. The quiet one… watch out).

MIKE…
(King of coffee driver guitar color, a blues man).

PEARL JAM…

Fate. Quickness. Hard work. No talk. No hype.

The coming together of 10.
…hands… eyes… ears…

with coitus & gold-E & a deep bench in N.Y. and L.A.
the journey begins.
Like your favourite plant… just add water.
Watch Pearl Jam grow.

The real story, of course, was a little more complicated. It begins and ends in Seattle, the latest city to have the world's attention focused on its indigenous music scene. According to legend, it's the home of slackers, a city of grunge rockers, a bottomless seam of talent. It's the home of Pearl Jam, and their ancestors… Green River, Mother Love Bone, Temple Of The Dog. It's inspired philosophical reflection, media hype, even a note of hysteria and jealousy. And the entire concept of a Seattle sound baffles those who supposedly created it.

Ask Pearl Jam guitarist Stone Gossard: "People have called it grunge, but I don't know what that means. I can't relate to grunge." Or perhaps Kim Thayil, of Pearl Jam's friends and fellow Seattle rockers, Soundgarden: "Grunge is a really neat word. It was a good marketing term; it has a nice ring to it."

But what does it mean? Here's American rock pundit Grant Alden: "The 'Seattle Sound' is only vaguely about music. The shock, for the rest of the world, seems to be in discovering the rage of a generation expected to go gently into the good life…

waking up one quiet morning and hearing that anger spewing over the radio, the same disenfranchised wrath voiced in hard-core rap, the same fury that boiled over in the Rodney King riots, only voiced by underground musicians who come from different musical and ethnic traditions. Nirvana, Alice In Chains, Soundgarden, Pearl Jam, Mudhoney ...they've all risen from the shoals of a stagnating culture like some great unkempt beast. And, to their shock, they found that their alienation was broadly shared."

Maybe Mudhoney, hub of the Seattle rock scene in the late 80s, more central to any local 'scene' than anyone, including Nirvana, said it best. "Everybody loves our town," they sang. "That's why I'm thinking of leaving it. It's so overblown."

Escape the catch-all media retrospectives and Seattle looks different. What gave the town its unity was its geographical position...Marooned at the North-West of the United States, closer to Canada than rock centres like California; its climate, cold, wet and unwelcoming; its feeling of being outside not just the mainstream of American youth culture but on the very borderline of America itself. Writer Tom Robbins has wisely pointed out that Seattle and the State of Washington as a whole are located as far away from Washington DC (the seat of the US government and home of the FBI, CIA, military and all law enforcement agencies) as it is possible to get, and it therefore attracts the kind of people who prefer to live as far away as possible from such regulatory institutions.

The US rock business is still centred on the California/New York axis. Seattle grew up without considering that it could ever influence what happened on either coast. As soon as the initial wave of Seattle grunge bands conquered America, that naïve, carefree vibe was lost...

for ever. And that's why every local luminary will tell you that Seattle is dead…even though its clubs are overflowing with identikit bands, and sheep-like A&R men, all searching for a second Nirvana, or Pearl Jam.

Beyond a town and (briefly) a record label, there's little to link Pearl Jam to Nirvana, who were primarily responsible for the commercial buzz that broke over Seattle. But to Mudhoney, still regarded by most as the conscience of the Seattle scene, there are much closer ties.

Teenage bands add and shed members as often as they change clothes, and it's only in retrospect that anyone wants to know who was where at any particular time. In the case of Pearl Jam, it's a complicated story, but it goes something like this.

In the beginning there were The Ducky Boys, The Limp Richards and Mr Epp. Three bands inspired to play variations on hardcore punk by the usual Seattle influences of UK new wave and American metal. The Limp Richards were the jokers in the pack, ruled more by the spirit of pastiche than by passion. Their contribution to the saga was Mark Arm, the creative centre of Mudhoney, and one of the instigators of the whole Seattle scene. Bizarrely, he was playing drums in the Limp Richards and simultaneously guitar in Mr Epp. Another Limp Richard was guitarist Steve Turner, who split his life between these comedians and the more

serious Ducky Boys. And it was that band who introduced the world to another Seattle guitarist, one Stone Gossard.

By 1983, The Ducky Boys had disappeared to the great garage sale in the sky, and briefly Stone Gossard vanishes from our story. The Limp Richards survived until 1984: that year, Steve Turner joined Mark Arm in a twin-guitar Mr Epp, while at the same time Steve formed another band, Spluii Numa, with fellow Limp Richard, Charles Guain.

Late that year, there was another merry-go-round of personnel changes: and with them, the formation of the key band in the lineage of Pearl Jam, Green River. Arm and Turner switched from Mr Epp to the new outfit, alongside drummer Alex Shumway from Spluii Numa and a newcomer to the family tree, Montana-born bassist Jeff Ament. Green River was the title of a single and album by Sixties San Francisco band Creedence Clearwater Revival, and the name of a North-West region of the States wherein lurked a particularly persistent serial killer, who'd taken 30 lives already and was never apprehended. Maybe he formed a grunge band as well.

Green River began to beg up support dates to visiting bands, and impressed Sonic Youth enough for them to insist on GR's presence on the bill whenever they were playing in the Seattle area. Sonic Youth left another influence on Green River... their sound, that fragmented, manic blend of punk and left-field imagery which was eventually named grunge towards the end of the decade.

Not every Seattle band on Green River's club circuit shared their Bohemian image. More local attention at the time went to the self-publicising, self-mythologising Malfunkshun whose mix of outrageous Seventies glam and punk, epitomised in the fey figure of frontman Andrew Wood, was difficult to ignore. Andrew (or L'Andrew The Love Child, as he insisted on being addressed) sported pancake white make-up, a silver suit, motorcycle boots with added platforms: he was, according to Sub Pop Records boss Jon Poneman, "a total rock star, even though he was the only person who thought so".

In 1985, the Seattle-based label C/Z issued 'Deep Six', a compilation album showcasing six local bands: hardcore pioneers The Melvins (philosophical mentors of the entire Seattle scene), The U-Men, Skin Yard, Soundgarden, Green River and Malfunkshun. Produced by Jack Endino, who assured his own immortality, if not necessarily wealth, by handling the sessions for the debut albums by Nirvana and Mudhoney, and a weighty proportion of releases on Seattle label Sub Pop, 'Deep Six' catalysed the town's alternative rock scene. As Chris Cornell of Soundgarden put it, "With 'Deep Six' coming out, we all said, 'Yeah, this is a way cooler scene than anywhere else'."

By the summer of 1985, Green River had added another guitarist: Stone Gossard, last seen escaping from The Ducky Boys, which allowed

Mark Arm to make the switch from guitar to vocals. It was this line-up that issued the band's first solo record, on the Boston-based Homestead label, which thanks to its links with distributors Dutch East Trading Company, ensured that the 'Come On Down' mini-LP would be available in Britain as well as across America.

Green River rarely stood still for more than a few months, and the release of 'Come On Down' was quickly followed by the departure of Steve Turner, who jettisoned cult success for the chance to join the true inheritors to The Limp Richards' role as Seattle court jesters, The Thrown Ups. Later, of course, he reappeared in Love & Respect, before eventually regrouping with Mark Arm in Mudhoney.

His replacement was guitarist Bruce Fairweather, establishing the Green River line-up that would see them through another year or so of intermittent conflict and local success.

Every Seattle rock success story eventually lands in the same place: with Jonathan Poneman and Bruce Pavitt, co-organisers (not that organisation was their strong point) of Sub Pop, undoubtedly the most important and influential US record label of the 1980s. It started out as Pavitt's baby, first as a fanzine, then as a vehicle for compilation cassettes of local bands. There was an LP, 'Sub Pop 100', in 1986; then, a year later, an EP by Green River and a single by Soundgarden, followed by an immediate cash crisis. Enter Soundgarden's manager, Jon Poneman, with a wad of dollar bills: "We started the company on about $19,000. We spent it on space, a little bit of advertising, and on putting out those two records."

Their joint enthusiasm was contagious. "Jon Poneman and Bruce Pavitt were the first people that ever told me that this scene was going to be huge," Soundgarden's Chris Cornell recalled. And with their insistence on limited edition releases, coloured vinyls, and strict quality control, they soon refashioned Sub Pop from a tiny indie label into a cult.

Recorded in June 1986 but not issued until Pavitt had scraped the money together in July 1987, the five tracks on Green River's 'Dry As A Bone' EP epitomised the original, no-holds-barred, Seattle sound. Sub Pop made the most of their marketing skills. There was an initial run pressed with a begging-to-be-collected yellow insert, then another run with a pink insert, and so on. And as much as any album recorded between 'Deep Six' and Nirvana's 'Bleach', 'Dry As A Bone' alerted the outside world to what was happening in the most obscure corner of America.

The same month that 'Dry As A Bone' reached the shops, Green River began work on what was supposed to be an album. They cut a speedy version of David Bowie's 'Queen Bitch', and then set out on a batch of original material, all composed by the Gossard/Fairweather/Vincent collective, with lyrics added by Mark Arm.

By the time that the 'Rehab Doll' mini-album was completed early in 1988, the band had disintegrated. It was their ethos which sparked the final battle: as Mark Arm told it, "It was punk versus major-label deal". The band who, according to Bruce Pavitt, had "destroyed the morals of a generation", collapsed after a show at the Scream Club in Los Angeles. Arm wanted backstage passes for their friends; Jeff Ament had already offered them to record company A&R men, who didn't bother to turn up for the gig. Arm split, accusing Ament of putting cash first, principles a long way after. After that, the Green River ran dry.

'Rehab Doll' eventually surfaced in June 1988 as an obituary for the band; while various Sub Pop and C/Z retrospectives and compilations dragged together the fragments of the corpse one more time. With the death of Green River, we kiss goodbye to the elusive spirit of grunge: the path from 1987 to Pearl Jam in 1993 scarcely touches on the sound which is supposed to be the unified voice of Seattle.

After Green River, there was Mother Love Bone, which was anything but a continuation of the past. There were three survivors from the old band, Stone Gossard, Jeff Ament and Bruce Fairweather. With Alex Shumway electing to work in a movie theatre, Gary Gilmour (no relation to the notorious murderer, incidentally) took over the drumstool. *Plus ca change*, you might think, except that Mother Love Bone's vocalist was the irrepressible Andrew Wood, fresh from scandalising audiences in Malfunkshun.

Wood, by all accounts, was a legend in his own brief lifetime. An eclectic, daring lyricist, his unique vision twisted the sound of the band into his direction. Stone Gossard remembered: "Any word Andy liked, he'd work into a lyric in some strange way. He was a very amusing guy, constantly putting on a show. He's absolutely one of my favourite lyricists of all time. If he could have been anybody, he'd have loved to have been Freddie Mercury. But Andy was misunderstood in a lot of ways, and in the same way Mother Love Bone has been totally glamorised."

Wood might have emerged as the face of Seattle; but he died of a heroin overdose in March 1990,

which is all that most people know about him. What's always ignored is his talent, immediately recognisable on Mother Love Bone's debut EP 'Shine', issued through Mercury in 1989, and on the album that was about to be released the week Wood died, 'Apple'. Chris Cornell, a close friend of Wood and the rest of Mother Love Bone, found the entire episode difficult to grasp: "When I went to his funeral, there were tons of people there who didn't know him, who were just, like, fans, and they were coming up to me and saying how they knew how I felt and how awful it was. It was really ridiculous. I mean, they didn't know how I felt, they didn't know anything. They were just rock fans going to a show. And the idea that Andy was perfect is pretty laughable. He had a lot of serious problems, like we all do. But something about a person dying, especially someone in the entertainment business, always elevates who they were and what they did into this other space."

Mother Love Bone's manager, Kelly Curtis, was as unaware as anyone that Wood was living on a short fuse: "I had no idea that Andy was as screwed up as he was until he died. I knew that he was struggling with it, that he'd gone to rehab. But he'd been straight." His death prompted a slew of rumours around the Seattle music industry, fingering any number of local luminaries as users. Some of these stories, as Nirvana know only too well, even reached print.

One person who didn't fall for the Mother Love Bone myth, of perfect creativity crushed by tragic accident, was Steve Turner, former colleague of Ament and Gossard, and a definite follower of the Mark Arm school of independent thought and distribution. "Look at Mother Love Bone," he carped. "They started at pretty much the same time we did in Mudhoney, but instead they went for

the major label golden carrot. A year later they had gotten a scrappy little EP out and were spending most of their time sitting at home talking to lawyers...and we'd already travelled around the world. A year after that, we had a few records out and had travelled around the world a couple more times. By that time, all they got to do was one scrappy promo tour and their singer was dead."

June 1990: Andrew Wood had been dead for three months, 'Apple' in the shops for two, and Polydor decided to drop the remaining members of Mother Love Bone. In any case, the group had already folded. That month, Soundgarden's Chris Cornell, who'd shared an apartment with Wood, wrote two songs about his friend: the elegaic 'Say Hello 2 Heaven', and the dream-vision, 'Reach Down'. Unwilling to lose the songs in Soundgarden's hard rock cauldron, he approached Jeff Ament

and Stone Gossard to help him record some demos. Matt Cameron of Soundgarden was roped in for the project, while Gossard brought along another guitarist, his schoolfriend Mike McCready.

Meanwhile, Ament, Gossard and McCready (with assistance from both Cameron and Dave Krusen on drums) were assembling a set of instrumental demos. What they needed were lyrics, and a singer with the vision to replace Andrew Wood without duplicating his sound. "For Pearl Jam I wanted a singer as much the opposite of Andy as I could find," Stone explained. "People think you only get one shot at finding a great singer, but fuck that, I don't buy that theory." He could say that with hindsight, as a chance connection introduced him to a Californian called Eddie Vedder.

Eddie's traumatic background has already become a legend, the more so as he never quite explains the full nature of the trauma. It was real enough, though: "I was a pretty weird kid, I guess. Probably because there was other shit going on in the house that I didn't want to deal with, I'd lock myself in the bathroom."

He fell out of school with no qualifications, and drifted into a series of no-hope jobs, but somehow he maintained the strength to educate himself; reading books, playing guitar, thinking about his past and how to overcome it. 1990 found him on the run from a band called Bad Radio, "mostly because of the lack of ambition on the other members' parts," and working the nightshift at a gas station. In the mail one day came a message from Red Hot Chili Peppers

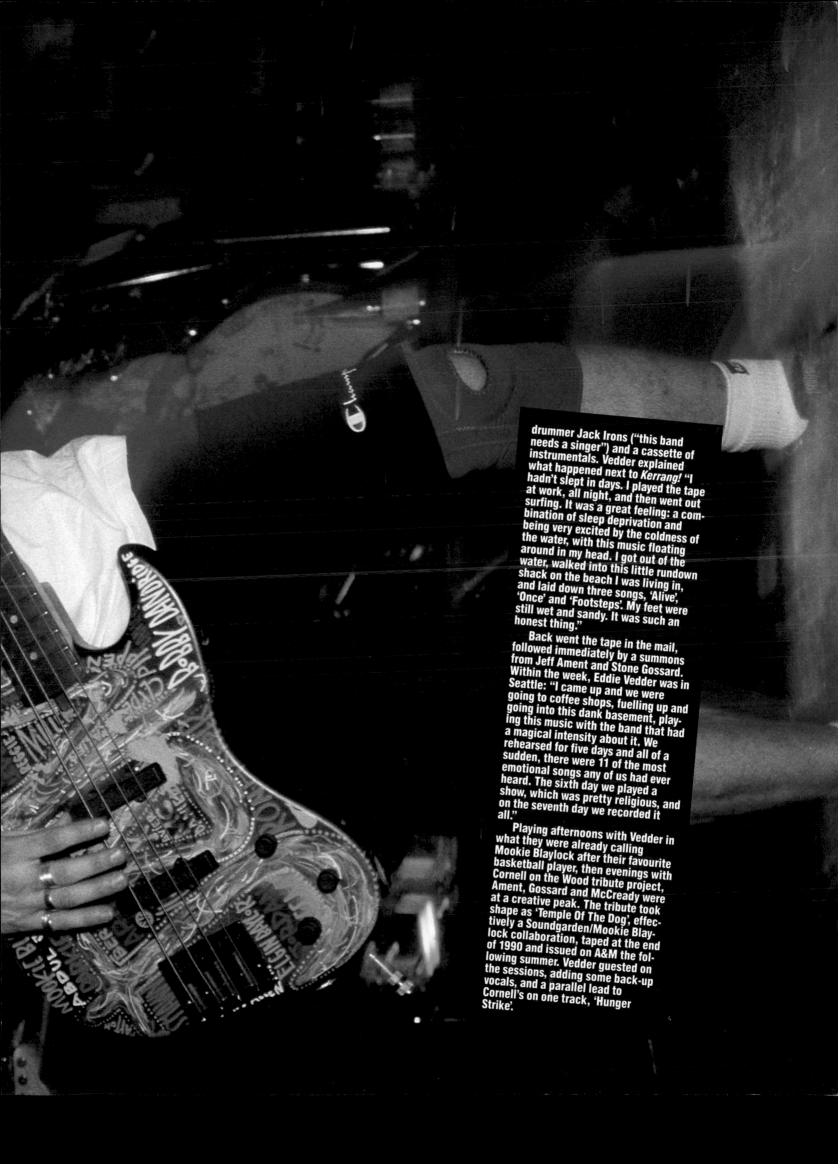

drummer Jack Irons ("this band needs a singer") and a cassette of instrumentals. Vedder explained what happened next to *Kerrang!* "I hadn't slept in days. I played the tape at work, all night, and then went out surfing. It was a great feeling: a combination of sleep deprivation and being very excited by the coldness of the water, with this music floating around in my head. I got out of the water, walked into this little rundown shack on the beach I was living in, and laid down three songs, 'Alive', 'Once' and 'Footsteps'. My feet were still wet and sandy. It was such an honest thing."

Back went the tape in the mail, followed immediately by a summons from Jeff Ament and Stone Gossard. Within the week, Eddie Vedder was in Seattle: "I came up and we were going to coffee shops, fuelling up and going into this dank basement, playing this music with the band that had a magical intensity about it. We rehearsed for five days and all of a sudden, there were 11 of the most emotional songs any of us had ever heard. The sixth day we played a show, which was pretty religious, and on the seventh day we recorded it all."

Playing afternoons with Vedder in what they were already calling Mookie Blaylock after their favourite basketball player, then evenings with Cornell on the Wood tribute project, Ament, Gossard and McCready were at a creative peak. The tribute took shape as 'Temple Of The Dog', effectively a Soundgarden/Mookie Blaylock collaboration, taped at the end of 1990 and issued on A&M the following summer. Vedder guested on the sessions, adding some back-up vocals, and a parallel lead to Cornell's on one track, 'Hunger Strike'.

By the spring of 1991, Ament, Vedder, Gossard, McCready and Krusen were ready to play live shows around Seattle. Managed by the same woman who'd handled Mother Love Bone, Kelly Curtis, they began sharing bills with another of her clients, metal merchants Alice In Chains. As the Seattle buzz began to grow, they attracted A&R men from the major labels. Epic won the toss, and by the late summer, the band were ready to cut an album.

First, they needed a name. Mookie Blaylock was cute, but an in-joke. They replaced it with another in-joke, but this one had resonance. Pearl Jam sounded impressive: what Epic didn't know was that it was taken from Vedder's grandmother, Pearl, and her finest recipe, a fearsome jam which supposedly had hallucinogenic qualities.

"Our first record was almost our sophomore record," Stone Gossard noted in 1992. "We had no time to make it at all." But it didn't show. 'Ten' (named, of course, after the number on Mookie Blaylock's shirt) was a staggeringly professional, inspired piece of work. Like 'Apple' and 'Temple Of The Dog' before it, it swept past any narrow preconceptions of the way Seattle grunge was

supposed to feel, creating an immediate classic rock sound that felt as if it had been brewed for years, then let loose at the optimum moment.

Most impressive was Eddie Vedder's entry into the big leagues. Guesting on the tribute album was a laugh; writing and then carrying a potential gold record was something else entirely. 'Ten' revealed that Vedder was a vocal stylist to match any exemplar you cared to mention ...Paul Rodgers, Steve Tyler, even Robert Plant...and also a lyricist of rare insight and honesty. Without descending into self-pity, he paraded his own demons across songs like 'Jeremy' and 'Alive', and made them universal.

The instrumentalists matched him all the way. McCready and Gossard's twin guitar passages were breathtaking. All the more so as they never overshadowed the core sound of the band, or dragged the songs into muso showcases. And Ament and Krusen's rhythm section provided a solo bedrock, Ament's bass lines sounding as fluent and occasionally off-the-wall as his distinctive sleeve-notes and artwork for 'Temple Of The Dog' had been.

December 1991 was the month that 'Ten' was released, and entered the US charts. Around the same time, Dave Krusen left the band, and was replaced by drummer Dave Abbruzzese. In January, with their debut single, 'Alive', already a staple on MTV, they re-recorded another album track, 'Even Flow', and cut some more new songs... 'Dirty Frank', 'Breathe' and 'State Of Love And Trust'. The last two were intended for the soundtrack of *Singles*, a film with a screenplay written by former *Rolling Stone* writer Cameron Crowe which had been in the air for nearly a year, and was in the final stages of shooting.

Set in the Seattle grunge scene, but not actually of it, *Singles* was a lightweight, though endearing, teen romance. Its locations may have been genuine, but its preppie characters were a long way removed from the nihilism of Seattle's underground. From the start, though, several members of Pearl Jam had been earmarked for the project, as Jeff Ament explained: "Me and Stone met Cameron about four years ago. I was just kind of excited, because he was a writer I used to read. At the time, Stone and I were working in coffee houses and trying to get Mother Love Bone off the ground. I heard from him a couple of years later and he got me to help out with graphics and art design, and then he wrote parts into the script for Stone and Eddie, who we'd just met. We probably shot for about 10 days to get 10 seconds of screen time."

Mark Arm, rumoured to be the model for Matt Dillon's leading role, slyly insisted that Dillon was closer to Jeff Ament, and the fact that Dillon was seen in the movie jamming with Stone Gossard lent some support to the theory. Three of Pearl Jam scored cameo roles, as the members of Dillon's amusingly named grunge combo, Citizen Dick. As it turned out,

what could have been a vital publicity boost wasn't required by the time
the movie was premièred.

In the States, the band had been
out on the road with the Chili
Peppers and Spinal Tap. Now, in
February 1992, it was time to hit
Europe. The album and single were
held back to coincide with the tour,
and Pearl Jam were introduced to
Britain in Southend, and then at the
Borderline, a breathe-in-and-you-
might-squeeze-in showcase venue in
central London.

Epic Records planned the show as
an industry jaunt, and the crowd was
dominated by label and press people.
What they didn't expect were real
fans, some drawn by the Nirvana
hype, others by having discovered
Mother Love Bone or 'Temple Of The
Dog'. While insiders swaggered in,
the fans were left in the cold. Horri-
fied, Eddie Vedder and Dave
Abbruzzese mingled outside, handing
out free promo CDs and apologies.
Despite that, the band still got the
stick from reviewers who'd been
allowed in for free. *Melody Maker*
made one perceptive remark: their
man reckoned Vedder was 'way too
fragile' for the superstar circus.

Audience response in Scandinavia
came close to terrifying the band;
back in England at the end of the
month, it was hatred rather than love
that was the problem, when Eddie
was catcalled by bigots for intro-
ducing 'Deep' as "a song about
homosexuality". They ended their

debut tour at the University of London. Vedder diving deep into the audience, before the band dissipated their triumph with an aimless encore jam with their support act. Pencils were already being sharpened for the backlash.

No matter: 'Alive' topped the specialist metal charts, while 'Ten' was outsold only by the new LP by Love & Hate. A week later, though, the *NME* went in search of the new Nirvana, and found not Pearl Jam, but Pavement. Keith Cameron wrote: "Watch Pearl Jam and you see a bunch of raggle-taggle cool street guys equating sensitive with wanking their guitars. It jars something rotten, and it's hard to decide whether to feel contempt or pity." His attack stung Vedder into an angry response when the band returned in June. Pearl Jam's credibility wasn't helped when Kurt Cobain lent his considerable public weight to the controversy, denouncing Jam as "a corporate band", jumping on Nirvana's bandwagon. Jeff Ament maintained his cool, and simply reminded Cobain that before Nirvana, there had been Green River.

Meanwhile, the re-recorded 'Even Flow' was readied for release in April. That month, Pearl Jam headlined at the Limelight in New York,

encoring with Neil Young's 'Rockin' In The Free World' and The Beatles' 'I Got A Feeling'. And 'Ten' finally outstripped 'Nevermind' in the US metal charts, *en route* to outselling that album worldwide over the whole of 1992. No wonder Kurt was miffed.

Two months later, the band were back in the UK, supporting The Cult 'In The Park'...London's Finsbury Park, to be exact. That was when Vedder let rip about the band's principles and passion, after being told about the *NME* story minutes before the show: "When I got on stage, I said, '*NME* says we're trying to steal your money. Don't buy the record, tape it off your friends. In fact, I hope there's bootleggers here who can make tapes and sell them. We want you to make money off this band. . . we don't give a fuck!"

Unfortunately, he did give a fuck, and the pressures were mounting on all sides. In June, the band prepared for a free concert in Seattle's Gasworks Park, designed to boost the 'Rock The Vote' campaign to persuade young people to register for the forthcoming presidential election. Three days before the show, Mayor Norm Rice pulled the plug. Eddie Vedder was distraught: "We knew we could easily deal with however many people turned up, but the Mayor and his people didn't agree. But it wasn't the *number* of people that bothered them, it was the *type* of people – 30,000 *young* people, 30,000 *alternative* people."

Back in Europe, there were some tempestuous shows in Scandinavia, before two dates in London. Pearl Jam never got that far. In Denmark, Vedder collapsed with what was described as chest cramps and exhaustion, though the official story denied that.

There were several problems. Vedder had been hassled by security men after stage diving in Roskilde; in Stockholm, the band's dressing-room had been raided, and he'd lost a notebook containing two years' of lyrics and stories. Mostly, it was their schedule: too tight and too tough. As Jeff Ament explained, "There were a couple of guys who felt that the whole thing was in danger of becoming not fun anymore. We called those shows off because we were in serious danger of burning out. The last couple of shows we played weren't as focused as we wanted. The vibe was totally angry and aggressive, not the vibe we usually have, and we felt it would be unfair to play for the fans that way."

Looking back on those events a few months later, Eddie Vedder filled in the details: "I felt totally raped, I lost my mind. And then I got home, and found out that one of my friends, Stefanie, from Seven Year Bitch, had died of a heroin overdose. And that kind of put me in a tailspin." Small wonder that Mudhoney's Mark Arm noted in August: "Eddie Vedder is real strung out at the moment".

Life carried on. There was an *Unplugged* show for MTV, where Eddie had the words 'Pro-Choice' scrawled on his arm, and *Saturday Night Live*, where the band were awe-struck at meeting sex goddess Sharon Stone, and Eddie sported a 'No Bush 92' T-shirt. The cameras backed off as soon as they caught that one.

Then came the Lollapalooza II tour across America, where Pearl Jam played alongside the Chili Peppers, Ice-T, Ice Cube, Ministry...a synthesis of rap and rebel rock, plus some freaky sideshows, all of which divided the media attention so much that Pearl Jam got off lightly.

A flurry of record company marketing ideas also switched the spotlight off the band, without lower-ing their commercial profile. A&M repromoted 'Temple Of The Dog', and this time they were able to boast Soundgarden and Pearl Jam involve-ment on the cover. Meanwhile, Mercury revived Mother Love Bone, combining the band's entire output on two CDs, with a previously un-issued track, "lacklustre and unauthorised," according to Jeff Ament, called 'Lady Godiva Blues'.

Writing in *Kerrang!*, Ament exposed mixed emotions about the whole deal: "Re-hyping something that's three years old doesn't seem right or fair to the fans who were there at the time. The one positive thing about this is that Andy made some amazing music, and it's cool that people are getting to hear it. My advice? Tape it from a friend, or buy the original versions, or steal it!"

With all things Pearl Jam tearing up the charts, the time was right for 'Jeremy', the band's third single. "It's a good story," Eddie Vedder said. "A kid blew his brains out in front of his English class. That probably happens once a week in America. It's a by-product of America's fascination, or rather perversion, with guns." But there was more to the song than that, as Stone Gossard noted: "Some of the inspiration for 'Jeremy' came from a Texan newspaper article, but you can tell that some of the elements are out of Eddie's own experience."

Before the pressure cooker went off, Pearl Jam had planned to have their second album in the shops for Christmas, or January 1993 at the latest. During the year, the schedule went back, and back. Stone Gossard was looking forward to when the band could return to Seattle for more than a stopover between tours: "There aren't a lot of distractions up here. Because we didn't have the record company hanging over us, bands develop based on playing music in clubs. We have more honest priorities – we make music because it's fun." And to prove his point, he began work on a project titled 'Shame', drawing in two musicians from local band Bliss, one of whom had once worked alongside Andy Wood in Malfunkshun. Meant to be more danceable than 'Ten', 'Shame' wasn't meant to endanger Pearl Jam's future, merely to keep Gossard from growing stale between albums.

With Shame set for release in March 1993, and Pearl Jam's sessions for the same month, the band could relax their way into the New Year at the Academy Theater in New York, where a support slot behind

Keith Richards turned into an all-star end-of-show jam with "Keef" and Robert Cray. Pearl Jam retained their reputation for eclectic cover versions; the Dead Boys' 'Sonic Reducer' and Ted Nugent's 'Stranglehold' turned up in their show, although the latter was undercut by Vedder's pronouncement that "Ted Nugent is a bigot!".

After little more than a year at the top, Pearl Jam, and especially the mercurial Eddie Vedder, had time to take stock. Eddie, being Eddie, had taken his responsibilities to his fans seriously, and was being hassled as a result: "I'm still that fucking surfer gas station guy who plays music. So I write fans back a normal letter and find myself becoming part of their lives, a part that they need, and they keep needing more and more."

It was a degree of passion he found easy to understand, as he shared it in his own life: "I've never really written for people, just for myself. And the fact that anybody, anywhere, has responded to this at all is very surprising. In an unexpected way, it's gratifying. I don't mean to sound all soapy and stuff, but coming from a pretty troubled past, it makes something so positive like this more overwhelming. If it weren't for music, I wouldn't have survived any of it. That's why the stakes are so high with me – music's everything."

Releasing a follow up to a debut album of 'Ten''s magnitude is not necessarily an enviable task, and the sophomore album's delayed release date may have spelt trouble to a few doubting critics. However, when the powerhouse called 'VS.' finally arrived in October of 1993 it turned out to be well worth the wait; the album debuted at Number One on the charts and sold close to one million copies in its first week.

'VS.' showcased a much tighter and more experimental outfit than the fledgling group that recorded 'Ten' with such explosive creativity. Eddie, Stone, Mike, Jeff, and Dave toured for a staggering eighteen months after the release of 'Ten'; playing together every night honed the skills of the musicians individually and made for a much more cohesive whole. Naysayers were unable to support their predictions that the band would churn out another album-ful of "arena rock" and attempt to ride the wave of 'Ten''s triumph with a clone before grunge and the Seattle sound became last year's gig.

'VS.', from the very first beat of opening track 'Go' featuring Dave Abbruzzese's funk drumming, demanded to be listened to in its own right; here was the sound of a band that had developed and grown.

The album was produced with Brendan O'Brien, who, according to Mike McCready, "can play every song ever written." O'Brien came to the band with extensive studio work under his belt – including producing the likes of Stone Temple Pilots and The Black Crowes – along with the distinction of having played lead guitar on Mick Jagger's *Wandering Spirit* album. He encouraged the band to set up as they do when playing live to record 'VS.'

Evidence of the pressures felt by Vedder and the band since becoming public property were easily found on 'VS.', not least in the cover artwork featuring a pissed-off and fed-up looking sheep, its teeth bared and eyes screwed shut as it attempts to break through a wire fence. Vedder's lyrics, perhaps more obtuse or more intensely private than on 'Ten', inevitably seemed to voice some of his frustrations. In 'Drop the Leash', he screams "Get out of my lucky face;" in 'Rearviewmirror' declares "I'm not about to give thanks or apologize."

Driven fury and complexity were not without their contrasts on this album, however, and the gentle, almost folksy 'Elderly Woman Behind the Counter in a Small Town' is a prime example. Vedder's trademark brooding baritone is tender and wistful here as he sings uncharacteristically straightforward lyrics; indeed, he seems almost free of the angst that often drives his voice to incoherence. In its January 1994 issue, *Guitar Player* magazine cited "cool rhythmic cadences that suggest Jim Morrison informed by Jamaican dub" in Eddie's vocals on 'Rats'. It was definitely an album of many diverse musical styles; as Mike McCready told *Guitar Player*, "We're just exploring different directions and combining our influences."

It was with what *Rolling Stone* magazine called a "grand 'fuck you'" that Pearl Jam refused to produce a music video to support their new album. This unprecedented act of rebellion was the beginning of what was to become a full-scale attack by the band against an increasingly commercialized music industry.

In April of 1994 Kurt Cobain killed himself. The man who had been crowned the King of Grunge by the media and who had become the reluctant spokesman for a generation's ennui and despair bowed out, leaving behind a wife, a daughter, and a community of fans and fellow musicians who all felt that nothing would ever be the same. Pearl Jam was two weeks away from completion of their tour; Eddie Vedder remembered being told by someone in a hotel room of Kurt's suicide. Eddie told *Rolling Stone*, "I couldn't believe he took the step. But I didn't think it was wrong, I just couldn't believe he did it. And I still

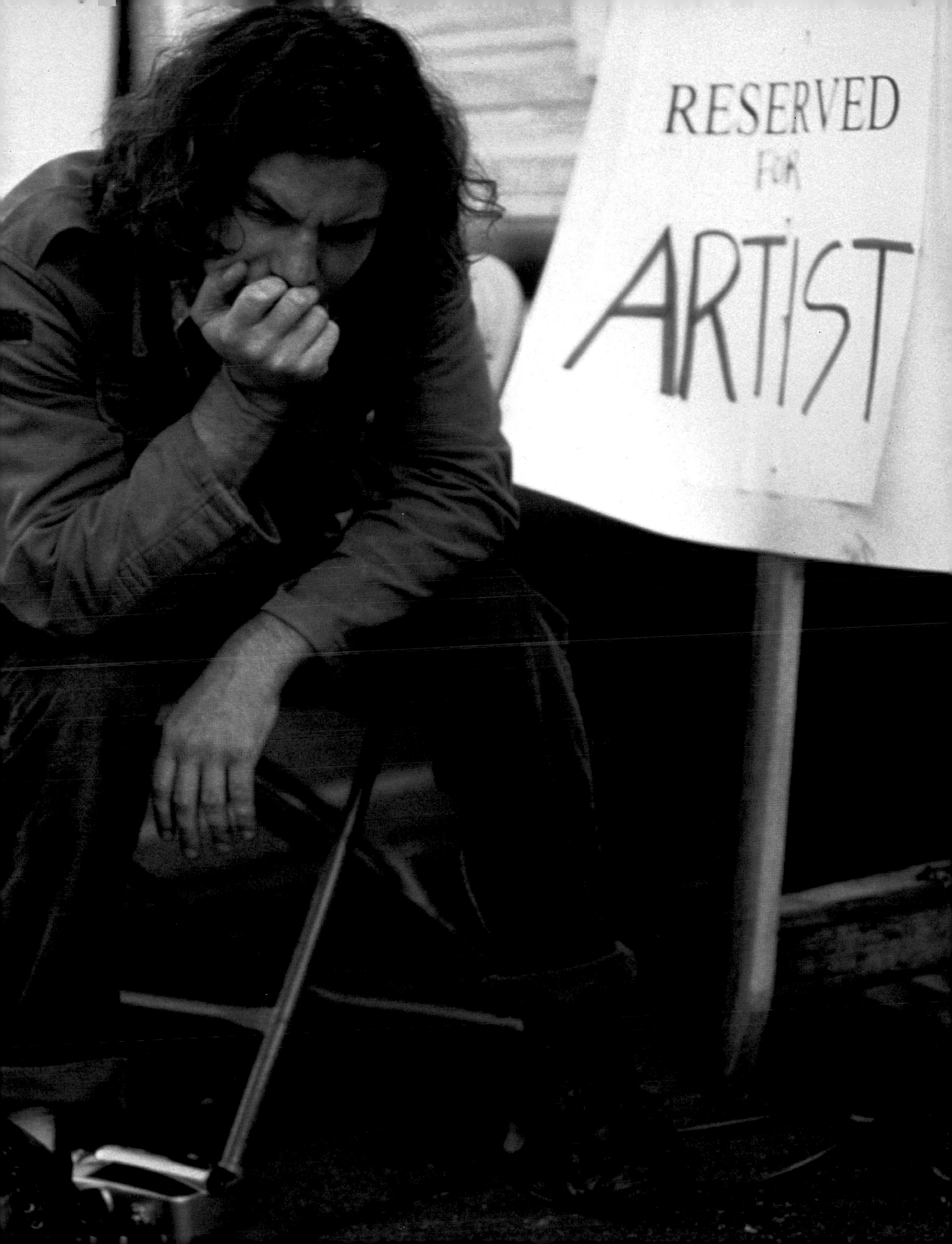
RESERVED
FOR
ARTIST

can't. After it happened, I wrote him a letter and asked, 'What's on the other side? And is there room for me?'" Eddie decided that Pearl Jam should complete their tour with the determination that once they'd done that they'd never have to play again.

On June 3, 1994, Eddie Vedder married his long-time girlfriend Beth Liebling in Rome. Although Beth's name would surface in the music press occasionally in the years to come, it would be almost exclusively due to her own band's activities; Eddie's resolve to keep his personal life as private as possible would not waver. Aside from a few publicity photographs of the couple in their wedding gear, little was disclosed about the ceremony or the newlyweds' past, present, or future – not for Eddie and Beth the high-profile, high-drama relationship of Kurt and Courtney.

Pearl Jam were to gain both praise and criticism in the coming years for their declaration of war against the giant U.S. concert promoter Ticketmaster. The band, disgusted at Ticketmaster's high service charges which well exceeded 10% of ticket prices, claimed that the agency had a monopoly on the sale of concert tickets nationwide. The band's escalating battle reached all-new and all-serious heights when Pearl Jam filed an anti-trust suit against Ticketmaster with the U.S. Department of Justice. In what must have been a true first on Capital Hill, Jeff Ament and Stone Gossard spent three hours testifying to government officials to the effect that the computerized ticketing service set ticket prices too high for young music fans.

Pearl Jam was backed by many other acts including R.E.M., the Grateful Dead, Neil Young, and Garth Brooks. Aerosmith's manager Tim Collins also testified at the hearings, quoting lead singer Steven Tyler as saying, "Mussolini may have made trains run on time but not everyone could get a seat on those trains." Regardless of fellow musicians' support, it was and is to this day Pearl Jam's war. The question remains as to whether the band is effectively shooting itself and its fans in the foot through this campaign. At times the band's refusal to play venues serviced by Ticketmaster has virtually crippled their touring ability. Many have queried whether it might be worth the asking price as the alternative seems to be no opportunity for fans to see the band live at all. As Pearl Jam manager Kelly Curtis said, "It would be impossible for us to do a normal tour without Ticketmaster. But that means Pearl Jam will probably never do a regular tour again."

Pearl Jam stubbornly contends that there is a principle at stake. As Eddie Vedder told *Rolling Stone*, "We don't want to exclude anybody from the experience. The experience of a father taking his son to the concert even though he works at a gas station... or even being able to afford a T-shirt. What music can do to your life, what one night of live music, if all the elements are in place, how it can effect your life."

'Vitalogy', the band's third album, was released on December 6, 1994. It sold in excess of one million copies before December 13th. It seemed that the band had weathered the storm of "overnight success," had survived the many self-inflicted

restrictions they'd put upon themselves and had passed the test: the album was greeted with almost unanimous critical acclaim and was declared Pearl Jam's "best record to date" by *Rolling Stone*.

'Vitalogy''s environmentally-friendly packaging houses a curious booklet combining song lyrics with what appear to be excerpts from predominately old literature on subjects such as "health and happiness," nightmares, "self pollution," family harmony, and marriage, along with a copy of a petition to President Clinton to take action against anti-abortion demonstrators. One article, entitled "Life Prolonged Indefinitely," puts forth that "If you permit no thought of disease and death to enter your mind you will have accomplished nine-tenths of the battle to stave off these foes." This noble sentiment, seemingly in tune with the combination of vitality and virology from which the album's title may possibly have sprung, is bizarrely followed by, "Tight clothing must of course be absolutely discarded." Well, Pearl Jam have certainly been accused of taking themselves too seriously on more than one occasion.

Indeed, the fourteen songs on 'Vitalogy' combine to present a near-perfect whole. Almost all of the album's tunes were written during the 'VS.' tour and were recorded in Seattle, Atlanta and New Orleans; in the midst of the transience and pressures of touring, the band seemed to have gathered their creative and musical energies to concoct an irresistible brew. Featuring full-on tirades done as only Pearl Jam can do them (the ode to vinyl of 'Spin the Black Circle' and the rage-driven 'Not for You') the album also includes compassionate ballads, and even a bit of silliness in the form of an accordion-based ditty called 'Bugs'. At once the simplest and saddest two tracks on the album, 'Nothingman' ("Could have been something/Nothingman") and 'Better Man' ("She dreams in color, she dreams in red/Can't find a better man") were written by Jeff and Eddie respectively.

In January of 1995, Eddie Vedder attempted to bring the Seattle community together again – if only for a jam session in his own living room – after the disintegration of the microcosm that began with Nirvana's overnight popularity and which avalanched after Kurt's suicide. The "jam session" was actually broadcast live worldwide; Eddie had arranged the event through KNDD 107.7 FM, a Seattle radio station. Pearl Jam, Soundgarden, Mudhoney, and Mad Season all played live and Chris Novoselic, formerly of Nirvana, gave a poetry reading. It was befitting of Eddie's persona to organize something at once private and public by allowing fans to witness and enjoy the gathering.

The ever-enigmatic frontman was not, however, completely "together" himself. In the *Rolling Stone* issue of that same month he confessed to being "way too fucking soft for this whole business, this whole trip. I don't have any shell." He also said, "I'm worried about everybody else, and I'm absolutely just a fucking mess myself," and "I still feel like we're that band everybody hates."

Pearl Jam is nothing if not prolific. In the midst of recording not only albums-full of original material but many B-sides along with the traditional Christmas singles sent exclusively to fan club members each December, the members of the band have, throughout the years, found the time to conceive and take part in an almost unbelievable number of side projects, collaborations, and "guest" performances. Eddie has contributed his inimitable voice to albums by the likes of Recipe for Hate and Bad Religion; he has also sung live with the surviving members of The Doors for their Rock and Roll Hall of Fame induction and with Roger Daltrey and Pete Townshend. Eddie and McCready performed at the Bob Dylan 30th Anniversary Concert and their version of 'Masters of War' appears on the tribute album. Eddie was to be linked at the end of 1995 with Porno for Pyros and engaged in a brief stint of playing drums for his wife Beth's band Hovercraft. His most recent outside venture was a duet with Pakistani singer Nusrat Fateh Ali Khan for the *Dead Man Walking* soundtrack. The

'Stone Free' Jimi Hendrix tribute album features a band called M.A.C.C.; this is in fact Jeff Ament and Mike McCready. Aside from these and many other one-off musical ventures, members of Pearl Jam have also spawned full-fledged bands with their own album releases. Mad Season is actually Mike McCready, Layne Staley of Alice in Chains, and members of The Screaming Trees. In 1996 Mike would form yet another band called Bumrush. Stone Gossard has his own band named Brad (who released an album entitled 'Shame'); his own Seattle recording studio Litho Studios; and his own record label called Loosegroove. Jeff Ament lent his bass chops to an album by his "side band," Three Fish.

Pearl Jam is also renowned for the diversity and abundance of songs they've covered. Amongst the ever-growing list is 'Driven to Tears' by The Police, Cyndi Lauper's 'Girls Just Wanna Have Fun', Chrissie Hynde's 'Brass in Pocket', along with tunes from The Beatles, Bob Marley, Talking Heads, Elvis Presley, Neil Diamond, and Bob Dylan. It was, however, Pearl Jam's signature encore – first presented on the 1992 Lollapolooza Tour – of Neil Young's 'Rockin' in the Free World' that brought about the band's most famous and perhaps most ambitious collaboration. Pearl Jam's version of the rock anthem was obviously to Young's liking. After a number of performances together over a few years' time, the grandfather of alternative rock and that now-established genre's hottest new institution joined forces to record 'Mirrorball', Neil Young's 1995 album.

Young flew to Seattle and settled right in with his new backing band; the entire album was recorded in just four days in January and February at Bad Animals Studio and was produced by Brendan O'Brien. All of the songs on 'Mirrorball' are credited to Neil Young; Eddie Vedder's creative input is limited to "additional lyrics" for the song 'Peace and Love'.

The project began quite innocently; Young suggested that he and Pearl Jam record a song entitled 'Act of Love' which they had performed together at the Washington, D.C. "Voters for Choice" concert. The musical partnership proved to be so right and so ripe that the group also recorded three other tracks Young had brought along in his overnight bag. After returning home, Young, duly inspired, penned the album's remaining seven tracks, returned to Seattle, and wrapped up the recording along with an exclusive concert for the Pearl Jam fan club.

The collaboration would carry on – with both a scheduled tour and various "surprise" appearances, including Neil Young coming to a flu-stricken Eddie Vedder's rescue at a near-aborted Pearl Jam gig in San Francisco's Golden Gate Park. Young has been widely quoted as referring to Pearl Jam as older than himself, explaining that "they've got old souls," and told *Guitar World* that the two factions share a mutual respect. "I think they're doing a great job. They like what I've done in the past and the fact that I'm still doing it. We're sympathetic." Mike McCready said, "We're enamored of him . . . and I'm honored he says he's into us."

What next? 'No Code,' Pearl Jam's fourth album, was released on August 27, 1996 and debuted at no less than Number One. The first single, 'Who You Are' - a mellow, hypnotic, Nusrat Fateh Ali Khan – influenced tune – gave fans a taste of the ever-evolving sound they were to hear on this latest effort. 'No Code' seems the perfect title for this loose, "no rules" collection of experimental and diverse songs. As *Rolling Stone*'s review put it "If you can't put out a glorious, guiltless, mad-blend mass of tunes and weird tangents like *No Code* when you're at the top, what's the point of swimming through all the sewage to get there?"

The album's artwork is an outward manifestation of the music within; a feast for the eyes, it features scores of colorful and apparently unrelated images.

These photographs, actually polaroids taken by band members and friends, are a visual echo of 'No Code''s songs, each its own snapshot of sound, separate in time and place from the others.

Indeed, with this truly compelling release, Pearl Jam, with new drummer and percussionist Jack Irons, seems to have decided that multiplatinum status and years of experiencing the best and worst fame has to offer does earn you a bit of creative license; after all, they've always contended that it was all about the music. Drawing from many musical influences and styles (most immediately apparent in the Neil Young – esque 'Smile'), here is an album at once eclectically derivative and uniquely inventive.

Not all critics are impressed by the "new" Pearl Jam. *Entertainment Weekly* called 'No Code' the band's "sloppiest, least cohesive work" and is not pleased with Eddie Vedder's lack of fury on the album, likening "Pearl Jam without pain" to "Seattle without rain." It is, however, Eddie's more spiritual outlook that most informs his lyrics here. In 'Present Tense' he wonders, "Are we getting something out of this/All-encompassing trip?" And it is his newly understated, wistful vocal style on many of the album's tracks that brings the power of his trademark roar to full effect on others.

By expanding their own boundaries, they have proven that they are a band that will endure. They don't always play by the rules, conform to the norm, or take heed of expectations, but they certainly haven't let us down yet. It seems that Pearl Jam is destined to continue to confound and delight us with their own brand of music for years to come.

ALBUM DISCOGRAPHY

GREEN RIVER: REHAB DOLL
Forever Means / Rehab Doll / Swallow My Pride / Together We'll Never / Smilin' And Dyin' / Porkfist / Take a Dive / One More Stitch
Sub Pop SP 15, 1988

MOTHER LOVE BONE: APPLE
This Is Shangrila / Stardog / Champion / Holy Roller / Bone China / Come Bite the Apple / Stargazer / Heartshine / Captain Hi-Top / Man of the Golden Words / Capricorn Sister / Gentle Groove / Mr. Danny Boy / Crown of Thorns
Stardog Records, 1990

TEMPLE OF THE DOG: TEMPLE OF THE DOG
Say Hello To Heaven / Reach Down / Hunger Strike / Pushin' Forward Back / Call Me Dog / Times of Trouble / Wooden Jesus / Your Saviour / Four Walled World / All Night Thing
A&M 395350, 1991

PEARL JAM: TEN
Once / Even Flow / Alive / Why Go / Black / Jeremy / Oceans / Porch / Garden / Deep / Release / Master / Slave
Epic 4688841, 1992

PEARL JAM: VS.
Go / Animal / Daughter / Glorified G / Dissident / W.M.A. / Blood / Rearviewmirror / Rats / Elderly Woman Behind the Counter in a Small Town / Leash / Indifference
Epic ZK 53136, 1993

PEARL JAM: VITALOGY
Last Exit / Spin the Black Circle / Not For You / Tremor Christ / Nothingman / Whipping / Pry, To / Corduroy / Bugs / Satan's Bed / Better Man / Aye Davanita / Immortality / Hey Foxymophandlemama, That's Me
Epic EK 66900, 1994

NEIL YOUNG: MIRROR BALL
Song X / Act of Love / I'm the Ocean / Big Green Country / Truth Be Known / Downtown / What Happened Yesterday / Peace and Love / Throw Your Hatred Down / Scenery / Fallen Angel
Reprise 9 45934-2, 1995

PEARL JAM: NO CODE
Sometimes / Hail, Hail / Who You Are / In My Tree / Smile / Off He Goes / Habit / Red Mosquito / Lukin / Present Time / Mankind / I'm Open / Around the Bend
Epic EK 67500, 1996